591.51   Flegg, Jim
Fle
         Animal hunters

DATE DUE

591.51   Flegg, Jim
Fle
         Animal Hunters

                              11.90

DATE DUE	BORROWER'S NAME	ROOM NUMBER

Animal Hunters

Wild World

Animal Hunters

by Dr. Jim Flegg with
Eric & David Hosking

Newington Press

FRONT COVER: A LEOPARD RESTS BETWEEN HUNTING TRIPS.
BACK COVER: A KESTREL BRINGS FOOD FOR ITS YOUNG.
TITLE PAGE: A PUFFIN WITH ITS BEAK FULL OF FISH.

First published in the United States in 1991 by Newington Press
2 Old New Milford Road
Brookfield, Connecticut 06804

First published in Great Britain in 1990 by Belitha Press Limited

Library of Congress Cataloging-in-Publication Data

Flegg, Jim
Animal hunters/Jim Flegg with Eric & David Hosking. Brookfield, Conn.: Newington Press, 1991.
32 p.: col. ill.; cm (Wild world)
Includes bibliographical references (p. 29)
Discusses the hunting skills of wild land and sea animals, such as the polar bear, tiger, hunting dogs,
heron, tawny owl, snake, chameleon, whale, leopard seal, shark, piranhas, dragonfly and wasp.
1. Animal attacks—Juvenile literature.
2. Aggressive behavior in animals—Juvenile literature.
3. Animals—Food—Juvenile literature.
I. Hosking, Eric John.   II. Hosking, David.
III. Title   IV. Series
ISBN: 1-878137-04-2   591.51

Words in **bold** are defined in the glossary.

Masai tribesmen hunting in Africa.

Contents

Animal Hunters 7

Polar Hunters 8

Underwater Hunters 10

Long-Legged Fishermen 14

Tiny Killers 16

Biological Control 18

Chemicals and Camouflage 20

Solitary Strategists 22

Pack Hunters 24

Aerial Assassins 26

Glossary 28

For Further Reading 29

Index 30

Animal Hunters

With the exception of a few small tribes living in the remotest areas of the world, people have more or less given up hunting other than as a sport. But for the jungle tribes of South America and New Guinea, the San people of the Namib Desert in Africa, the Aborigines of the Australian Bush, and the Inuit (Eskimos) of the icy Arctic wastes, hunting is still important. Meat provides essential fat, protein, and vitamins in their diet.

Humans are more suited to a life of herding and farming. They do not have the excellent senses of sight, hearing, and smell on which the animal hunters of the world depend for their survival. Our hunting instincts may appear, though, in times of war when we need to defend ourselves from enemies or make counterattacks. And, of course, we have our mechanical and electronic tools. Our natural senses and skills have been improved by technology—missiles, aircraft, radar.

The hunting skills to be found in the animal world can stand comparison with anything our technology has developed. The leopard would surely beat the commando in stealthy approach, and birds can fly far better than any aircraft. Hunting dogs have a team discipline that would be admired by any troop of soldiers. The sight and hearing of the owls, and the heat-sensing ability of many snakes, would be envied by soldiers in night combat. The breathtaking speed and deadly accuracy of the falcon are as effective as any missile in striking its target. In this book you will discover how hunters of the wild world use their senses, instinct, and intelligence to keep ahead in the battle for survival.

A peregrine falcon and prey.

Hunting dogs outside their den.

A polar bear on the Arctic ice fields.

Polar Hunters

The polar bear is a hunter of immense power. Living year-round in the icy wilderness of the Arctic, it leads a largely solitary life. It is the most northerly and perhaps the loneliest animal on Earth. Hunting is the major feature of the life of a polar bear. Although seabirds may be caught during the brief Arctic summer, these count as little more than a snack. The main item in the polar bear's diet is seals, particularly the ringed seal. The polar bear lies in wait, often for hours, pressed flat close to a break in the **ice floes** or beside a seal's breathing hole in the ice. When the seal surfaces to breathe, the huge polar bear strikes with amazing speed. Such is the strength of the bear that it can pull a ringed seal right out through a hole no bigger than the seal's head in ice often several yards thick. This forcible digging out can break or dislocate most of the bones in the seal's body, as the bear drags it out onto the ice before it can sink back out of reach into the icy sea.

At around 10 feet (3 meters) long, the leopard seal is one of the largest seals. Its thick layer of insulating blubber beneath its skin helps it to withstand the icy temperatures of the Antarctic Ocean as it swims deep into the **pack ice**. In summer, leopard seals will feed on *krill*—the incredible masses of shrimplike creatures that some whales also love to eat. But the leopard seal is primarily a **predator,** as its powerful fangs show. Young pups of other seals are easy prey during their first few days in the water. Leopard seals will often eat penguins, too. These the seals catch by lying in wait offshore, near the ''landing stages'' of rock or ice that the penguins regularly use on their way to and from their nesting colonies. Swift and agile in the water, the leopard seal uses its long whip-like neck to advantage. It can easily snap up an unwary penguin, which it will shake to bits before gulping it down.

A leopard seal basking in the Antarctic sun.

A brook lamprey showing its suckerlike mouth.

Underwater Hunters

The lamprey is in many ways a living fossil. It is one of the few remaining animals belonging to one of the earliest of all groups of vertebrate (backboned) animals. These were primitive fishes without jaws and first appeared about 400 million years ago. Lampreys have a life history with two distinct stages. The first is as a small **larva,** living buried in the mud of freshwater streams and filtering tiny food particles out of the water. The second stage, the adult, is about 12 inches (30 centimeters) long, eel-like, and usually lives in the sea. Here it seeks other fish and will fasten onto one with its huge, muscular, suckerlike mouth. With a tongue like a rasp, it cuts away the flesh of its victim to feed on its blood, an easily digested meal. The flow of blood is controlled by the lamprey's saliva, which contains an **anticoagulant** to prevent blood clotting.

The fearsome jaws of the great white shark.

The great white sharks can rightfully claim to be the super-**predators** of the world's oceans. Seals and turtles are their favorite prey—and it takes little imagination to see how alike a human swimmer is in silhouette, especially paddling on a surfboard. The powerful jaws of the great white can bite a swimmer in half. Perfectly streamlined, most of its body is solid muscle. The great white packs the biggest attacking punch of any predator. Amazing senses allow it to pick up and identify distant swimming movements and even heartbeats. Blood in the water can be detected from several miles away. Just before it strikes, the shark opens its jaws, gaping half a yard (half a meter) or more across, revealing dozens of daggerlike teeth. Its eyes roll back in their sockets for protection. Great whites are renowned for their ferocity and will even attack a steel-hulled boat.

A school of piranhas on patrol.

Possibly even more terrifying than the sharks, the freshwater piranhas are much smaller than their competitors for the title of "most feared fish." A member of the tigerfish family, the piranha lives in the sluggish backwaters of South American rivers and rarely exceeds 12 inches (30 centimeters) in length. What they lack in size, they make up for by ferocity and teamwork. Piranhas operate in schools often hundreds strong. Renowned for their huge appetites and bad temper, they attack anything in their path with powerful jaws and razor-sharp teeth capable of snapping a steel fishing line. Other fish, water-loving animals, and even drinking cattle can be reduced to skeletons in a matter of minutes. In 1819, an entire troop of soldiers trying to ford a river were devoured by these voracious hunters.

The anglerfish, or monkfish, is a large, ugly, bottom-living sea fish. Its appearance is dominated by its huge mouth, lined with rows of sharp teeth. These are sharp enough to slice straight through a careless fisherman's rubber boots. Lying mostly concealed by sand on the seafloor, the anglerfish uses its bait or lure—a specially adapted **dorsal fin** spine—to tempt likely fish victims within reach. On the end of the drooping spine hangs what looks like an interesting morsel of food. If curious fish venture too close, the huge mouth opens and shuts like a trap, securing the meal. In the ocean depths where daylight cannot reach, deep sea anglers need a lure that can be seen. Their lure is **phosphorescent** for this purpose.

An anglerfish with its partly eaten prey.

Long-legged Fishermen

The herons hunt by stealth. With great caution, they pace through the shallow water at the edge of a lake, causing hardly a ripple to disturb the fish that they seek. The long neck is carried partly folded, and once the **prey** is in sight the daggerlike beak stabs forward, reaching fish a surprising distance away. Purple herons have developed this technique even further. They are birds of warm, sunny climates and have to be careful that their shadows do not alert fish to their presence. The purple heron overcomes this hunting hazard by holding its feathers close to its body, reducing its outline to the minimum. It stretches out its beak, neck, and body toward the sun, so that the shadow cast is as small as possible. The shadow falls at the point where the bird's legs enter the water, where there is least risk of disturbing a fish. Specially adapted downward-swiveling eyes allow it to hunt efficiently, despite having its nose in the air!

A purple heron makes a successful catch.

14

A black heron shields the water with its wings as it hunts for fish.

Using exactly the opposite technique, the black heron seems to be just as successful a fisherman as its cousin the purple heron. The chicken-sized black heron lives beside shallow African freshwater lakes. It scampers along the water's edge before darting out into water only a few inches deep. There, it spreads its wings and arches them forward, looking just like a black umbrella. It will stand still for a minute or more. **Researchers** argue over why it does this. Some say that fish are tempted into the patch of shadow to escape the fierce heat of the sun. Perhaps more likely, the heron is shielding its eyes from the sun's blinding glare, reflected off the water. Using its wings much as we would use a hand to shade our eyes, it finds the fish and frogs sheltering in the waterweeds easier to spot and catch.

A dragonfly nymph lies in wait for its prey.

Tiny Killers

The female dragonfly hovers low over the lake surface in midsummer, dabbing the tip of her tail on the water to lay each egg. The **nymph** that emerges from the egg spends a surprising time under water—up to four years—breathing through gills like a tadpole. The slow-moving nymph is one of nature's most voracious and ferocious hunters and will attack **prey** much larger than itself. Lying in wait, hidden in the waterweeds, it uses its jaws, called a "mask," to grab passing prey like fish or tadpoles. The jaws are huge, much larger than the mouthparts of the adult dragonfly. They are folded like a spring under the head and shoot forward to grab the prey. When the nymph is mature, it climbs onto a reed stem while amazing body changes take place inside its old skin. Then it scrambles up the stem and out of the water. The skin splits, and the adult dragonfly climbs out. It spends some hours drying and pumps blood into its tightly folded wings to expand them before it can fly off—a beautiful but efficient insect **predator.**

Ant lions are the appropriately named **larvae** of a group of harmless-looking four-winged insects related to alder flies and lacewings. This larva is plump and up to almost an inch (2 centimeters) long, with short bristly legs. Most striking are its mouth parts, a pair of large curved fangs. These are sharp and powerful and have a groove running along their inner side, down which the body fluids of its **prey** flow into the ant lion's mouth.

Ant lions use ingenious traps to catch their prey of ants, beetles, and other insects. Each digs a pit with steep sides in sandy soil and hides buried in the sand at the bottom. Any unwary insect coming too close to the lip of the trap slips in. The sand is so loose that, try as it might, it cannot escape and is doomed to slither to the bottom to be seized in the ant lion's vicious jaws.

The trap of the ant lion (right) *is surrounded by dead ants.*

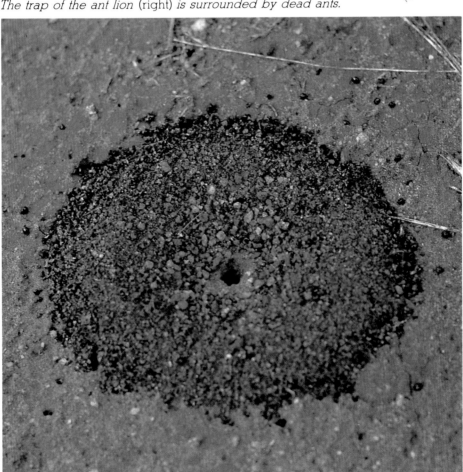

Adult parasitic wasp emerging from a whitefly.

Biological Control

As people become increasingly concerned about the harm **pesticides** may be doing to the environment and to themselves, scientists are turning more and more to nature to help in pest control. By encouraging the natural enemies of crop pests, the use of poisonous pesticides can be drastically reduced. Special **virus** diseases have been developed to kill codling moth caterpillars (the "worm" that often attacks apples). **Parasitic fungi** spread over aphids and kill them. Also in the biological control army are lacewing and ladybird **larvae,** which have a tremendous appetite for aphids. Parasitic wasps, much smaller than the jam-loving variety, seek out whiteflies, which are difficult to kill with insecticides. The wasps lay their eggs in them. The growing wasp larva eats the sluggish whitefly alive, from the inside. Emerging as an adult from the whitefly's remains, it flies off to seek fresh victims.

The ladybird larva has a great appetite for aphids.

The wood wasp uses its long ovipositor to lay its eggs inside wood-boring grubs.

No matter how dramatic its black-and-yellow-striped body, nor how long its "sting" seems to be, *we* need have no fear of the wood wasp. The "sting" is in fact its *ovipositor,* a slim, sharp-ended tube through which it lays its eggs. With supreme skill—probably by detecting minute vibrations—the wood wasp hunts for wood-boring beetle **larvae** that chew tunnels deep in timber. When it locates one, it pushes its ovipositor through the wood, also penetrating the larva that had seemed so safe in its tunnel. The wood wasp lays its egg inside the larva. When the egg hatches it develops *inside* the wood-boring insect, gradually eating it alive. Related to the useful honey-bee, these **parasitic** wasps are increasingly used as an alternative to **pesticides** to destroy damaging insects.

A grass snake opens its jaws wide to swallow a frog.

Chemicals and Camouflage

The **venomous** (or poisonous) snakes are equipped with an offensive weaponry that exceeds even the most unpleasant chemical warfare weapons developed by humans. Snakes use various types of **venom**: some affect the blood supply of their victims, others paralyze by crippling the nervous system. Some venoms have no known **antidotes** and may kill within minutes, even in the tiniest doses. All snakes, such as this nonpoisonous grass snake, have jaws that can be dislocated at will—so the mouth can open very wide. Some have hinged fangs, which lie folded back in the roof of the mouth until the strike. Then they flick forward and release the venom from storage pouches in the cheeks. In addition, the pit vipers have an infrared-sensitive, heat-seeking sensor that can detect nearby warm-blooded prey. This system rivals the heat-seeking sensors in our air-to-air missiles.

The chameleon can change color to match its background.

The chameleon excels in its use of camouflage. Normally greenish, chameleons can change color almost instantly over a range from yellow to brown and almost to black. In their skin are many small purse-like cells containing pigment, or coloring matter. These cells are able to respond automatically to change the skin color and camouflage the chameleon. Spotting its **prey** is easy for the chameleon. It has eyes that swivel independently—so it can actually look in two directions at once! Chameleons have a flexible bone in their tongue. Normally, the tongue is folded into the mouth like a jack-in-the-box. But when prey is in range, out snaps the tongue to trap the unlucky insect on its sticky saliva.

A common cuttlefish.

Cuttlefish are masters of the art of camouflage. Swift color changes allow them to match a sandy or rocky background where they can lie in wait for their prey. Their eight sucker-covered arms and two long tentacles can quickly wrap around prey even as formidable as a crab. The cuttlefish kills with a **venomous** bite from its parrot-like beak. If threatened, the cuttlefish pumps out a dense cloud of brown inky fluid. Hidden behind its "smokescreen," it sucks in water and pumps it out through a narrow tube called its siphon, and escapes by high-speed jet propulsion.

Solitary Strategists

Mature leopards live alone except when male and female come together to mate. Each roams a territory many miles square in dry bush and forest margins. Unlike lions, leopards hunt on their own, relying on speed, strength, and above all excellent camouflage to make a kill. Stealth is the key skill of the stalking leopard's approach to its **prey**. The leopard relies on good hearing and sense of smell to locate its victim. Its brown-spotted sandy coat provides a cloak of near invisibility as it creeps toward its prey, belly pressed as close to the ground as a snake's. The victim is seized by the throat after a sudden rush. Leopards are superb tree climbers and extremely strong. Often they will haul an antelope almost as big as themselves up into the branches. Here it will be safe from hungry scavengers like hyenas and vultures.

This leopard has hauled its kill into a tree for safekeeping.

An alert tiger lurks in the long grass.

Black, white, and orange stripes may not seem to be the best colors for camouflage. But in the fierce sunlight of an Indian jungle, where the canopy of leaves casts a pattern of alternating bright light and intense shade on reddish earth, they can conceal a tiger very effectively during the day. Although it hunts and kills at night—when silent stealth is vital but camouflage unimportant —the tiger needs to stay hidden during the day. If the antelope and deer feeding in its territory were to be frightened away, finding an evening meal would be much more difficult for the tiger.

After a successful hunt, the adult hunting dogs feed the pups.

Pack Hunters

Hunting dogs hunt in packs. The multicolored, blotchy coated animals are led by the biggest and strongest male, who will have several favorite bitches. The rest of the pack will usually be careful not to annoy this group. But when the hunt starts, rank is forgotten! Usually it will be a weak antelope (often a wildebeest or a gazelle) that is singled out as their target. Perhaps this will be an elderly or sick individual, or a youngster separated from its mother. Once started, the pursuit is relentless. However desperately the fleeing animal tries to escape, the pack of hunting dogs keeps up with its twists and turns. The pack changes its "pacemaker" lead dog so that the group can keep up full speed, sometimes for hours. The cornered victim is finally overwhelmed by a snarling mass of dogs, who dart in past sharp horns and flashing hooves. Once the kill has been made, members of the pack take choice chunks of meat back to the favorite bitches and their pups, safe in their underground den.

All the toothed whales are hunters, but most ferocious of all is the killer whale, or orca. Hunting in schools (called pods) of up to fifty, they cause panic among other marine animals. Seabirds and fish (even great white sharks) may be eaten, but the orca specializes in catching seals and sea lions, chasing them at up to 15 miles (25 kilometers) an hour. Pods of orcas will even hunt baleen whales, harrying one individual as hunting dogs hound a gazelle until it succumbs to exhaustion and multiple injuries. There are old tales of orcas herding other whales into bays where whaling ships were hunting, in return being thrown the massive tongues of any whales caught. This ability to cooperate with man may explain why such a ferocious hunter can become so tame and easily trained in captivity.

Killer whales are air-breathing mammals, not fish.

A tawny owl swoops down on a mouse with deadly accuracy.

Aerial Assassins

Most owls are nocturnal (nighttime) hunters, and the tawny owl is no exception. Large eyes, especially sensitive at low light levels, give eyesight ten times better than that of humans. Its eyes are so large that they cannot move within their sockets. The tawny owl must turn its whole head to look to either side. In fact, it can turn its head right around to look backward.

Experiments have shown that of all the owls, the long-eared owl has the most acute hearing. In total darkness, a long-eared owl was able to pinpoint and make a successful strike on a scuttling mouse over 65 feet (about 20 meters) away. Rustling feathers must not interfere with this keen hearing, so owl feathers have a special, velvety, sound-deadening surface. Nor must the owl's wings whoosh in the air as it swoops down. The leading edge has a comblike fringe that breaks up the air flow and silences the beating wing most effectively. A strike from eight lethal talons completes a successful kill. The two tufts of feathers on the head are simply for display. The real ears are huge, taking up half the owl's head, but are hidden behind the head feathers. The secret of the owl's keen hearing lies in the disks of feathers that give all owls their special face patterns. These act as reflectors, collecting and focusing the slightest of sounds into the owl's ultra-large ears.

A long-eared owl.

Watch the hunting kestrel, hovering head into the wind. No matter how strong the wind, or how much the wings beat and the tail twists to maintain the kestrel's position, the head is held rock steady. This, with the eyes for seeing and the brain for coordinating movements, is the control center that must remain still for a successful kill. At heights often

A kestrel brings a dead rat to its nesthole.

exceeding 100 feet (about 30 meters), it will use its phenomenal eyesight (probably ten times better than ours) to spot **prey**. This includes not just mice or voles, but also worms and beetles on the ground beneath it. When it plunges, talons outstretched, it often pauses halfway down to check that it is still on target.

The peregrine has for centuries been a favorite bird with **falconers** in places as far apart as America, Arabia, and China. Peregrines feed almost entirely on other birds. The larger female tackles prey up to goose size, while her mate takes prey like pigeons and golden plover. Peregrines have a unique hunting technique, circling silently high in the sky, waiting to ambush prey flying far below. Closing its wings, the peregrine dives headlong in pursuit. At full speed, this "stoop" may exceed 125 miles (over 200 kilometers) an hour. The bird strikes its target with its talons outstretched. Usually the impact brings instant death, and the peregrine can land to eat its prey.

A falconer with a peregrine falcon.

Glossary

anticoagulant a substance that prevents blood from clotting

antidote medicine given to fight poisoning or disease

assassin a person or animal that causes the violent death of another

dorsal fin a fin found on a fish's back

falconer a person who hunts using falcons or other birds

fossil the remains of a plant or animal that lived a long time ago—often found in rock

fungi (singular = fungus) mushrooms and similar plants, including molds, that live on other dead or living plants or animals

ice floes sheets of floating ice

larva (plural = larvae) the grub form of an insect, from the time it leaves the egg until it becomes a pupa (when it changes into an adult insect)

nymph the young form of some insects that resembles the adult insect but with the wings and other parts not fully developed

pack ice large areas of floating sea ice in the polar oceans, made up of a large number of *ice floes*

parasitic living in or on another plant or animal and taking nourishment directly from it, or depending on another plant or animal for nourishment. A plant or animal that lives like this is called a parasite.

pesticides substances for destroying pests, especially insects

phosphorescent giving off light in the dark without heat

predator an animal that lives by hunting other animals for food

prey an animal that is killed and eaten by another animal

researcher someone who looks carefully to find something out; an investigator

strategist someone skilled in working out a plan of attack

venom a poisonous substance produced by some snakes and other animals and used by them when attacking other animals or defending themselves

venomous an animal able to use *venom*

virus one of a group of extremely tiny disease-causing agents, possibly the very smallest living things

For Further Reading

A First Look at Owls, Eagles & Other Hunters of the Sky
 by Millicent E. Selsam and Joyce Hunt
 (Walker & Co., 1986)

Animal Attackers
 by David Taylor
 (Lerner Publications, 1989)

Animal Defenses
 (Time-Life Films, 1978)

Birds: The Aerial Hunters
 by Martyn Bramwell
 (Facts on File, 1989)

Bugs for Dinner?:
The Eating Habits of Neighborhood Creatures
 by Sam and Beryl Epstein
 (Macmillan, 1989)

Discovering Birds of Prey
 by Mike Thomas & Eric Soothill
 (Bookwright, 1986)

How Animals Behave: A New Look at Wildlife
 (National Geographic Society, 1984)

Index

A
Anglerfish (monkfish), 13
Ant lion, 17
Aphids, parasites of, 18

B
Battle for survival, 7
Biological controls, 18, 19
Black heron, 15

C
Camouflage
    of chameleon, 21
    of cuttlefish, 21
    of leopard, 22
    of tiger, 23
Chameleon, 21
Codling moth caterpillar, 18
Cuttlefish, 21

D
Dogs, hunting, 7, 24
Dragonfly nymph, 16

F
Falcon *see* Peregrine
Fossil, 10
Fungi(singular-fungus), 18

G
Grass snake, 20
Great white shark, 11

H
Herons
    see Black heron;
    Purple heron
Hunters
    Arctic, 8, 9
    camouflaged, 21, 22, 23
    flying, 26, 27

insects as, 16, 17, 18
    pack, 24
    solitary, 22, 23
    underwater, 10, 11, 12, 13, 25
    venomous, 20
Hunting
    animal skills in, 7
    to obtain food, 7
Hunting method
    of ant lion, 17
    of chameleon, 20
    of cuttlefish, 21
    of dragonfly numph, 16
    of great white shark, 11
    of herons, 14, 15
    of hunting dogs, 24
    of kestrel, 27
    of lamprey, 10
    of leopard, 22
    of leopard seal, 9
    of orca, 25
    of owl, 26
    of peregrine falcon, 27
    of polar bear, 8
    of tiger, 23

I
Insect predators, 16, 17, 18

K
Kestrel, 27
Killer whale (orca), 25
Krill, 9

L
Lamprey
    adult form of, 10
    larvae of, 10
Larva
    of ant lion, 17
    of dragonfly, 16

of lacewing, 18
of ladybird, 18
of lamprey, 10
of woodboring beetle, 19
Leopard seal, 9

M
Monkfish (anglerfish), 13

N
Nymph, 28
   of dragonfly, 16

O
Orca (killer whale), 25
Owls
   hunting skills of, 7
   long-eared owl, 26
   tawny owl, 26

P
Parasites, 28
   as biological controls, 18, 19
   of insects, 18, 19
Peregrine, 27
Piranhas, 12
Pit vipers, 20
Polar bear
   hunting method of, 8
   prey of, 8
Predators, 28
   flying, 26, 27
   insects as, 16, 17, 18
   packs of, 24
   polar, 8, 9
   solitary, 8, 22, 23
   underwater, 10, 11, 12, 13, 25
   venomous, 20
Prey, 11, 14, 16, 17, 21, 22,
   27, 28
   of ant lion, 17

of black heron, 15
of chameleon, 20
of cuttlefish, 21
of dragonfly, 16
of great white shark, 11
of herons, 14
of hunting dogs, 24
of kestrel, 27
of lamprey, 10
of leopard, 22
of leopard seal, 9
of orca, 25
of owls, 26
of peregrine falcon, 27
of polar bear, 8
of purple heron, 14
of tiger, 23
Purple heron, 14

R
Ringed seal, 8

S
Scavengers, 22
Shark, great white, 11
Strategist, 22

V
Venom, 20
Venomous snakes, 20
Virus, 28
   as biological control agent,
   18
   of codling moth caterpillar,
   18

W
Wasps
   parasitic, 18, 19
Whales, toothed, 25
Wood wasp, 19